LETTER TO A GODCHILD

BOOKS BY

REYNOLDS PRICE

LETTER TO A GODCHILD

BOOKS BY

REYNOLDS PRICE

REYNOLDS PRICE

LETTER TO
A GODCHILD

CONCERNING FAITH

SCRIBNER

NEW YORK   LONDON   TORONTO   SYDNEY

SCRIBNER
1230 Avenue of the Americas
New York, NY 10020

SCRIBNER and design are trademarks of
Macmillan Library Reference USA, Inc., used under license
by Simon & Schuster, the publisher of this work.

For information about special discounts for bulk purchases,
please contact Simon & Schuster Special Sales:
1-800-456-6798 or business@simonandschuster.com

Set in Electra

Manufactured in the United States of America

1   3   5   7   9   10   8   6   4   2

Library of Congress Cataloging-in-Publication Data
Price, Reynolds, 1933–
Letter to a godchild : concerning faith / Reynolds Price.
p. cm.
Includes bibliographical references.
1. Faith. 2. Christianity.
3. Price, Reynolds, 1933– —Correspondence.
4. Price, Reynolds, 1933– —Religion. 5. Voll, Harper Peck.
I. Voll, Harper Peck. II. Title.
BV4637.P7453 2006
230—dc22   2006042328

ISBN-13: 978-0-7432-9180-4
ISBN-10: 0-7432-9180-8

FOR

HARPER PECK VOLL

PREFACE

This book is the text of an actual letter addressed to the son of longtime dear friends. It was first intended as a brief gift at the time of Harper Peck Voll's baptism in the year 2000 in the church of Saint-Ferdinand des Ternes in Paris. I was not present at that baptism and am not a Roman Catholic, but Harper's parents were kind enough to let me assume the title of honorary godfather. For years now the child has lived some three thousand miles away; and while we've had occasional moments of telephone conversation — when Harper takes the phone from one of his parents — I've had to imagine from photographs what sort of person he's becoming.

From the sound of his growing voice and from my first actual memory of seeing him, I've proceeded to expand the initial letter. The first memory is simple but imposing. On the working theory that people are born, to a large extent, ready-formed in personality and character, I've leaned expectantly on the act Harper performed when — in my wheelchair (which he'd never seen) — I visited him and his parents in New York. He was only some eighteen months old; but when he glimpsed my rolling chair, he trotted across the large room and employed all his strength in pushing a long coffee table completely out of my way. No one had asked him to do it. From the start, I took that to be a hopeful sign — his clearing a space for me and the fact that, some months earlier, his first words had been *book* and *soap*. At widely separated intervals since the child's baptism, then, I've rethought the gift with slow enthusiasm and have continued to develop it in the intention of arriving at a document that would be genuinely helpful to a friend in his early adult years.

It has seemed feasible to me that, by describing succinctly, and as honestly as I could manage, the advancing line of my own religious life, I might provide a useful sense of how one person's existence shaped itself round an early inexplicable event and moved onward from there till now, the start of my eighth decade. The letter was not intended to be a child's book or even something an adult could read to a child, but I haven't convinced myself that such a gift was pointless.

When I myself was a pre-schoolboy, I received as holiday presents from my father's sisters a few volumes that at first proved incomprehensible to me — as words on a page, in any case; their illustrations were another story. I stood the books on my parents' bookshelf, though, and mostly thought of them as secrets waiting to unfold before me when I'd earned full access — that is, when I could read English sentences of some complexity. In its final form here then, *Letter to a Godchild* is a substantial communication from a family friend to a child who may someday wish, or need, to read it—perhaps in adolescence or whenever after (few things are more unpredictable than the age at which a particular text may communicate with another human being).

I hope also that numerous other growing children will find it of interest, and even good help, when they're ready to turn to something on this order. Parents themselves, hoping to rear strongly grounded children, might possibly read this account of one person's childhood and youth, and the faith that grew in those years, and gain further awareness of the conditions of environment and training which helped to sustain that man's faith through long decades with their inevitable devastations—physical, psychic, and intellectual.

Not at all incidentally, it's meant to be of potential use to young men and women who are not Christian and were not reared in such families. Christianity happens to be the tradition in which I first encountered the notion of a creating power in the universe—an awesome overarching power which appears to witness some of our lives, perhaps all our lives, steadily. But the same creative power which impels my own faith says in various other traditions—some of them far more ancient than Christianity—that it has not only certain expectations of human life but that it also offers perhaps bottomless wells of patience and compassion. The Christian tradition is the one in which I continue to acknowledge and negotiate with that Creator, though since my early twenties I've done so outside the walls of an organized church and in ways that might seem heretical to many.

This book, however, is not an attempt to convert anyone to the Christian faith. Far from it. In fact, I'm among the least evangelical souls alive. Thus I hope that *Letter to a Godchild* may find a place in the thoughts of persons who approach maturity in families that have reared them as Jews, Muslims, Buddhists, Hindus, Christians — or otherwise, or perhaps without religion altogether. The reality of a single Creator is literally beyond the scope of human description, in words at least.

Yet for those of us accustomed to Western traditions of contemplating ultimate mysteries, the greatest composers of music have offered extended glimpses in the spans of sublimity granted to Bach, Handel, Mozart, the late Beethoven, and the dying young Schubert — among several others (there is gorgeous earlier Christian music; and while I'm sadly deficient in my knowledge of Asian music, I've heard ragas from India that approach a comparable state of ecstasy; and I assume that there are other such moments of over-reach in the traditions of cultures unknown to me).

Despite the towering limitations on any verbal effort to communicate both the transcendence and the unpredictable approachability of the Creator, I hope that the assertions and questions offered here may prove helpful — not only to my friend Harper but to any number of

readers, especially those who find themselves riding atop baffling conventions (or their own private curiosities) and who hope to clear for themselves a navigable path through the endless and darkening thicket our lives so often seem to be.

RP

LETTER TO A GODCHILD

Dear Harper,

It will be some years before you read this, if ever. But given the uncertainties of all our futures in a violent time, I'll set these thoughts down here in your childhood in the hope that—should you ever feel a need for them—they'll be legible still and at least as comprehensible as most letters from the distant past. Chances are slim that you'll feel the need of any such reading for more than a decade. By then the twenty-first century will be thoroughly under way. And since it's likely to move as unforeseeably as the twentieth—just now it's scrawled with America's murderous war in Iraq and with radical Muslim violence on our doorsteps—I'll make no effort to predict how the world will feel about religious faith in your early manhood. Feelings on that ancient subject, here in America and even more so in Europe, are almost surely more complicated than they were in 1900 for instance (the year of my father's birth); and in many powerful quarters, those feelings are tending toward polar com-

I

plexities that surpass even those of a century ago in dangerous simple-mindedness, if not lunacy.

I certainly won't guess at what your own relations to any form of religious faith may be years from now, despite the fact that your parents and godparents vowed, at your baptism a few years ago, to guide you toward their own faith. Those watchful adults have old ties to churches, though the ties vary in nature from both Irish and French Catholic to German Protestant. Above all, none of us who knows you in the alert wonder of your laughing open-armed childhood can begin to imagine who you'll be and where you'll want—or, again, need—to go in your youth or your maturity. Here then, by way of what I offer as a belated christening gift, are some thoughts that may interest you in time. Let's say that they come, if not from a blood kinsman, from an honorary godparent then—one who's at least spent a good deal of time over seven decades in considering the matter.

As I write, near the start of this new millennium, a large majority of the world's population claim that they're religious. To turn to our own country, for instance, some 80 percent of the adult residents of the United States identify themselves as Christian—at least nominal associates in the world's most populous faith. Considerable numbers of other residents of the United States identify themselves as Jewish, Muslim, Hindu, and theistic Buddhists; and there are small numbers who adhere to smaller sects. What did each of those persons mean by his or her claim to the census taker? The *Oxford American Dictionary* says that *religion* is belief in, reverence for, and desire to please, a divine ruling power; the exercise or practice of rites or observances implying this.

Surely most thoughtful Americans would agree with the definition; and obsessive verbal tinkerer that I am, I'd suggest only one change. Instead of "divine ruling power," I'd substitute the more specific and descriptive "supreme creative power." I might also wonder if it wouldn't be desirable to strip the definition to its bones and say simply—"religion is the belief in a supreme creative power." After all, a great many human beings believe in such a power but, for whatever reasons, they neither desire to please it nor attempt in any way to worship it. Perhaps, though, such a stripped definition denotes the word *faith* more adequately than it does *religion*. The dictionary may be right to insist that religion itself involves a belief which results in reverence and worship.

I hope you'll be interested to know that I—at past the age of seventy now—am still able to believe, with no strenuous effort nor any sense of self-delusion, that the whole known universe was willed into being by an unsurpassed power whom English-speaking peoples at least call God. Whether there are other, and lesser, powers within that universe—a power or powers that we might call evil, for instance—I have no notion (I often suspect that there are). I believe, though, that the Creator remains conscious of his creation and sustains an interest in it. Most days I believe that his interest may be described, intermit-

tently at least, as love; and that's a matter I'll say more about below.

Incidentally, I say *his* with no strong suspicion that God shares significant qualities with the earthly male gender, despite the tendency of many religions to attribute to the Creator not only male gender but such male characteristics as impatience, ever-ready anger, and decidedly demeaning views of women. I also avoid capitalizing the male pronouns with which I refer to God here. That practice came late to written English; the early editions of the King James version, for instance, do not capitalize those pronouns.

Whether God's attentive to every moment of every human's life, as some religions claim (including my own), I'm by no means sure. There's a good deal of evidence that he isn't. But I do believe that God has broad standards of action which he means us to observe, whether he attends to us closely or not. I believe that he has communicated those standards—and most of whatever else we know about his transcendent nature—through a numerous and ongoing line of human messengers. He has likewise spoken to us through the mute spectacles of nature in all its manifestations, around and inside us, from the beautiful to the horrendous. The

---

◀ *The Grand Canyon provides anyone who hunts for faith on the face of our planet with a good deal of acreage—plus flora and fauna—for contemplation of the almost endless questions.* (Corbis)

human kidney, to take a single instance, is as intricate and ultimately impressive a masterwork as the Grand Canyon, perhaps more so.

God began to create his inhuman spectacles many billion years ago; and he began to send those human messengers, to this planet in any case, as long as four thousand years ago, maybe much earlier. And by *messengers*, I don't mean extra-planetary aliens. I'm thinking of parents and teachers, prophets and poets (sacred and secular), painters and musicians, healers and lovers; the generous and often celibate saints of Hinduism, Judaism, Buddhism, Christianity, Islam, and a few other faiths — the chief feeders of our minds and bodies. One of the matchless gifts of our present life lies in the fact that those messengers continue to come, though the task of distinguishing valid messages from the false or hateful or merely confused is hard, often dangerous, and unending.

I and most other Christians believe that at least one of those messengers was in some inexplicable sense a unique embodiment of God. It's to his name, and the loving work he commended to us, that you were recently dedicated in a great church by your elders. The Aramaic name by which he was known to his family in the first century of our era was Yeshua. In English we call him Jesus, a sound that might have startled him with its strangeness, though it's derived from the Greek *Iesous* in which his story first reached the world. The four gospels were originally written in Greek, though Jesus was born into a carpenter's family and spent most of his life apparently in an insignificant village in Galilee, a province in the north of the country which Rome called Palestine; and Aramaic, a language related to Hebrew, would have been his chief means of communication.

Finally, I believe that the essential core of our individual nature is immortal. In that belief I join a sizable majority of the human race, past and present, who appear to agree that there's imposing evidence that the core of each of us is immune from death and will survive in an eternal and conscious form. The central creeds of Christianity assert that, in some unspecified way, we survive in what Paul of Tarsus calls a "spiritual body" for all eternity. Despite the fact that most ancient Hebrew scripture expresses no firm faith in individual immortality—only some continuance in a place called Sheol, an underworld much like the Hades of Homer—later Jewish belief has sometimes claimed that the virtuous dead will be raised into a perfect immortality with the advent of the messiah. Hinduism and Buddhism believe in reincarnation, a more complicated version of the Western belief in immortality. Insofar as I understand its complexities, Eastern reincarnation hopes to end its cycles of rebirth—from existence as a venomous spider, say, to participation in the life of a single green leaf on a beech tree in springtime—in blissful utter extinction, all cares and all consciousness extinguished.

Most Christians believe that whether we'll experience eternity as good or bad is likely to depend upon the total record of our obedience to God's standards of action. Most of the long-enduring human systems of faith say that we slowly accumulate the weight of our wrongs—our sins, our "missings of the target" (which is the Hebrew meaning of the word *sin*), or our karma (from the Sanskrit word for action or fate). They also assert that we'll ultimately be confronted with that no doubt considerable weight. Some strands of the teaching of Jesus, for instance, suggest that we may be punished after death—and forever—for the worst of our failings. Other elements in his teaching, and those of his immediate followers, suggest that such a punitive accounting is far beneath the expansive nature and concern of a being so merciful and so all-saving as God, the father of all life.

For what it may be worth, I'll say that a wide lobe of my own brain finds it hard to believe that the maker of anything so vast and still so mysterious as our universe—and of who knows what beyond it—is permanently concerned with how I behave in relation to my diet (so long as I'm not a cannibal or a cruel killer of other edible creatures) or how I use my genitals for anything besides excretion (so long as those organs don't do willful damage to another creature, above all to a child) or how I wear my hair (so long as it doesn't propagate disease-bearing vermin) or with a good deal else that concerns and even distresses many religious people. I can understand a person's or a community's strict observance of certain codes for the purposes of discipline and tribal identity; but to attribute the establishment of such codes to the eternal and inalterable will of God seems to me a deeply questionable, if not an absurd, choice.

As for his firm expectations of me, I strongly suspect

that God cares how I treat the planet Earth, its non-human inhabitants, its atmosphere, and eventually outer space. Above all, the Creator intends that I honor the bodies and minds of my fellow human beings—whomever and from wherever—and that I do everything in my power not to harm them. I must likewise alleviate, as unintrusively as possible, any harm they suffer from others or from nature itself; and I must attempt to repair any harm that I may have done to others. I believe I know that my own grave wrongs have involved a self-absorbed indifference to the feelings and the mental stability of other human beings. Those errors have generally occurred in relations that involved erotic desire; and I've spent a fair amount of time, even now when paraplegia has severely curbed my scope, in contemplating those wrongs with real regret.

God likely expects me to extend the honor due my fellow humans to other forms of life, especially to other animals less powerful than I and therefore easily at my mercy (I think it's possible that God wants us not to kill or eat other conscious creatures—cattle, sheep, goats, perhaps fish—though I happen to be a restrained carnivore who feels no real guilt in that practice; still, I think I know how I'd feel if Martians landed tomorrow and began to hunt down me, you, and our families for food or slave labor). How far down the scale of life that honor is to reach, I don't know—surely I'm not meant to avoid killing by inhalation, say, a pneumonia bacillus, though some Jain monks in India wear face masks to avoid killing small insects.

Though I've mentioned that a preponderance of Americans presently share some version of my faith, it's fair to tell you that a likely majority of the social class I've occupied since my mid-twenties doesn't share those beliefs. I'm speaking of those men and women who've experienced extensive years of academic training and who hope to pass their knowledge onward. I'm always surprised, though, to learn how many of my writing and teaching colleagues at Duke University are devoted churchgoers. Nonetheless, a significant number of my colleagues hold no beliefs which might be called religious; and a few of them are articulate in expressing their incredulity that an educated person can believe in a creating mind, especially one who goes on attending to his creation.

That incredulity characteristic of many in the intellectual classes of the Western world and, say, of a good deal of Europe and China is more than a century old at the least. And their defection is largely the result of a few discoveries by the physical sciences and by the worldwide calamities of war which have convinced many intelligent and feeling witnesses that no just God can exist. Oddly, perhaps—and so far as we can now discern—such calamities in prior centuries served chiefly to intensify faith in the existence of a mastering intelligence beyond our own. The Lisbon earthquake of 1755 is famous for having been a great test of faith, and it may have been the first natural calamity to produce such a widespread effect.

*   *   *

My formal schooling, in America and England, lasted nineteen years. I've also read widely in the literatures of many cultures that are not my own. How then can I explain my rejection, in the matter of faith, of the doubts or the flat refusal of so many in my social class? In brief, how did someone as extensively trained as I sustain — with no significant doubts through a long life — a belief in God's existence and his consciousness of me? Is my persistence chiefly a symptom of mental blindness or of some other failure of plain intelligence? And am I suggesting that the reasons for my disagreement with so many of my otherwise admired friends should have any weight with you, when you face a crossroads of belief and rejection at whatever point in your life — certainly years beyond the point at which I write to you here? The outline I'll offer of the evolution of one man's beliefs is set down chiefly because it seems to me the description of a fairly unexceptional journey by someone fewer than thirty years older than your parents.

First, it's worth saying that I've by no means defected from all my peers. And I certainly take no preening pleasure in assuming the role of a lonely hero on the ramparts of mystical insight. Put plainly, a great many highly schooled men and women, known and unknown to me, have never agreed to accept the central rationalist dogmas of many in our caste. Fortunately and crucially, like most believers, I received the rudiments of faith well before I began to read or attend school, at least two decades before I began to teach in a secular university community. And while that faith has undergone assaults, from myself and others, it's never quite buckled.

To be honest with a fact that may seem surprising in a man who claims your at-least-respectful attention, I've occasionally been suspicious of the apparent durability of my convictions. Shouldn't anyone who's lived as long as I—on two continents—and who's traveled widely, who's known, revered, and occasionally loved so many elaborately educated non-believers, and who's sustained more than one maiming personal catastrophe—have undergone occasional dark and punishing nights?

Of course I have but they've been dark nights of the restless intellect, not of the parched or assaulted spirit. My own desert treks, like those of so many million under the wide hand of deep depression, have closely resembled the ordeals described by the Spanish monk John of the Cross in his prose and verse self-examinations. My reading and my observations of extensive melancholia in myself, my mother and her family, as well as in my friends and students, suggest that the internal ordeals of depressed believers differ from the mental sufferings of others in one large respect alone—often a literally life-saving respect. We may feel God's absence as a form of near desperation, and that pain may last a very long time; but it almost never tumbles us finally into outright disbelief, despair, and the entire absence of hope, which so frequently ends in suicide.

Note how I said above that, like most human beings, I *received* the rudiments of faith; I didn't mine them in solitude out of bedrock. Those early-arriving rudiments came from the usual sources—my parents and a few of my kin, the natural world around me (which was frequently rural or wooded suburban), and from God and his various messengers, by which I do not mean winged visitors companioned with uncanny lights and soothing music. To say that much, here and now, runs a heavy risk of pomposity, an absurd degree of self-love, and a ludicrous elitism. Yet I know of no more accurate way to describe a situation that, in simple fact, is—again, as I'll try to show—far from uncommon.

My preparation for faith likely began with something as uncomplicated as the gift of two Bible-story books—one was a collection of Old Testament tales from my paternal grandmother when I was two or three years old. The second came a year or so later from my parents and was *Hurlbut's Story of the Bible*. That latter volume was a remarkably unexpurgated retelling for children of all the narrative portions of the Bible. The two books, both of which are still with me, proved to be long-range endowments for the only child I then was (my brother was born only twelve days before I turned eight) and on through the last days of childhood. Each of the books contained strikingly realistic illustrations of outlandishly dressed but credible men, women, and children involved in plainly compelling actions.

So with a small amount of guidance from my parents, I launched myself on an early fascination with the prime characters and stories from Hebrew and Christian sacred texts—Abraham, Sarah, and Isaac; Ruth and

Naomi, David, Jonathan, and Saul; Samson and Delilah; Joseph, Mary, and Jesus; Jesus and the girl he raises from the dead, Jesus himself rising from the dead and greeting the friends who thought they'd lost him. My parents were prepared to buy me almost any book I wanted or which they thought desirable. But they seldom read to me, even when I could not read to myself.

That was a holdover, I suspect, from their own family traditions, when children were thought of as children, not as pets; but for me their own family traditions proved fortunate. Though I owned other good books in my childhood, nothing else made me long to read for myself more powerfully than the chance of learning those ancient and immensely pregnant stories on my own. Even now I don't know why, beyond the fact that there are no better stories—literally none in our culture which can promise a child both a more fascinating tale and a glimpse at least of the footsteps of God, the motions of his hands.

At about the same time, I began occasionally to go to church on Sunday with my father. My parents were not doggedly loyal church attenders; yet their own faith,

---

◄ "Moses Views the Promised Land," an illustration from a much-prized possession of my childhood, *Hurlbut's Story of the Bible*. In its refusal to hedge or sentimentalize the stories of Hebrew scripture, Hurlbut's unidentified artist portrays the great leader of the Exodus, foiled by God in his hope to enter the land he has fought so hard to gain for his people.

in my early childhood, seemed to be unquestioned by them. Thus in the several towns where we lived while my father pursued work in the Great Depression, I experienced occasional Sunday-school classes where I heard the prime Bible stories again in the company of other children and in rooms where we drew our own pictures of such striking heroes and made plaster-paste models of their houses and towns with the palm trees and sand which we imagined as their home country (when I first went to Israel in 1980, I was mildly surprised by a scarcity of sand). Through such early good luck then—and in the midst of a childhood whose interests were hardly focused on anything that might be called religion—I glimpsed the fact that those stories meant something important to many other men, women, and even a few children.

By the time I was eight or nine and had learned to read, I began to see—again, very much in my spare time—that none of the people in the stories seemed crazy or self-deluded by sweet fictions concerning God or their apparently normal visits from angels; and none of them do today, though in retrospect I can see what a blindly selective use we made of the stories of Jesus above all. As in most cultures, we retold the stories that served our own interests and passed over those that might have condemned some feature of our lives. My family and I lived in a society that was borne up in every particular by a sometimes benignly paternal but ultimately vicious repression of black Americans that any thoughtful child might have seen as bafflingly hypocrit-

from his origins and the family he may have left there (he once told me that he'd left a son named Felix).

My parents were only recently married and were in various forms of trouble, owing to Dad's drinking and the Depression; but Grant approached them for odd jobs, and they took him on. Mother told me "Sometimes we couldn't pay him, but at least we could always feed him." He was especially good at yard work and gardening; and when I was born in 1933, Grant folded me into a delightful brand of babysitting (by then he was near seventy, if not older).

In my infancy, when I'd just begun to walk, he'd spend occasional long evenings with me, playing his harmonica while I danced before him with a baby's awkward glee, then sharing his harp while I played and he danced. I can just recall my falling-down hilarity. By then Grant's younger woman had vanished for good, and he had come to care for my father—a mainly lovable man—who needed Grant's fire-tested strength. Though my parents were then strapped for funds, and in the domestic trouble I've mentioned, they were nonetheless near the peak of a social pyramid of which Grant lay under the base; yet Grant gave freely what Will Price needed—patient companionship when he was drunk and on the road in search of a bootlegger.

Neither of them ever recounted those times to me, and they're long since dead. All I have now is the little that Mother told me in my adult years and the powerful images I retain from childhood of the interdependence of those two men. I can clearly recall times when I was between six and eight and Grant came to live with us in a new house we'd built (he established our garden and tended our yard with a fierce but delicate genius). I also recall still later times, when he was a very old man and had returned to our native county, though we then lived ninety miles away. On return visits, Dad would take him a huge new battery for his primitive radio and sit with him for an hour's talk and laughter in his one-room house while I'd play in Grant's yard with his preposterous turkey gobbler.

I also recall that, on the night before my father underwent the radical lung surgery which resulted in his death a few days later, he told me that Grant Terry should be among the short list of close friends whom he wanted as pallbearers at his funeral. Neither of us had heard, by then, of Grant's death some four months earlier, at about ninety years old (he'd never been sure of his birth date). After Dad's death, I came to see that a mysterious healing spirit had been at work in my father's care for Grant and in Grant's care for him. Then and now, I've never doubted that the spirit was divine.

And while Dad died only a few months before the effective start of the civil-rights movement in America — and while he could have imagined no way to upend an entire way of life more than three centuries old, nor could he then have wanted it — that spirit had long been at work in him and thus in me, a devoted and attentive son. My mother lived to witness the movement at close hand; and she came to see clearly the monstrous racial error of her world and to begin repairing the final rifts in her own good heart, though she was near death by then.

Returning to my own early path, the next important gift for me — after my Bible-story books — came at about the time I began the first grade of public school. It was a beginning that provided the great excitement of my childhood (there had been no available nursery schools or kindergartens). We lived then, in the early years of the Second World War, on the edge of a small textile-mill town with only a few other houses near us; and one of the revelations of my early schooling was that so many of my classmates were the children of poor white mill hands. One boy in my second-grade class regularly came to school barefoot in the cold winter, and I took baffled notice of that.

Within roaming distance for me from our house were thickets of pine with plentiful birds, rabbits, foxes, possums, and raccoons; and there was a small stream filled with crawfish, toads, turtles, minnows, and snakes. I spent countless solitary and silent hours exploring that teeming world. And there I began to store up an invaluable sense of the endless inventiveness of life and the savage conditions of so much animal, not to mention human, existence. (Lucky as I was in my steadily kind parents, I first learned of human savagery from Bible stories, though a few members of my extended family would offer early and unforgettable examples of cruelty, and even physical violence, to the cousins with whom I regularly played.)

In those same woods around our home, I even uncovered and saved my first flint arrowheads from the vanished Indians who'd lived on that very ground centuries earlier. Through many long days I roamed the thickets imagining myself as the last local Indian, with fake redness daubed on my cheeks and a dime-store bow in my hands with a real flint point tied to my arrow. I found more than one of those beautifully shaped old stones at my feet in our woods; and their simple endurance helped me move further onward with their intimations of the doggedness, and yet the frailty, of human life. Three or four years earlier, I'd been given yet another important book—one called *Wigwam and Warpath*, which told unflinchingly how my own Bible-pounding forebears had driven the Indians from this very land and exterminated them in cold blood. The book made no pious or patriotic excuses; and reading it, even now, I'm startled by its honesty.

Then late one afternoon in the backyard of our house

◄ *This arrowhead was found for me by Grant Terry, a black man who may have been born a slave, in 1939 in the yard of a house we were building in Randolph County, North Carolina. Its elegant precision became at once, for me, a survival of the indigenous peoples of the area and an early witness—for a child who'd already fervently studied Indians—to a civilization far older than my own. As a boy of six, I saw its blunted tip as a casualty of warfare or, at the very least, of hunting. In any case, it has been on my desk ever since, an object imbued with usable power.* (Courtesy of the author)

in the country, still alone but blissful in that world, I was given a visionary experience. I was either six or seven years old (I know because of the place where we lived then—the house, the nearby woods and creek, a thick pine tree in the back yard). I've read a good deal about the resources of the human brain for amazing fantasy, benign or frightening or malevolent. But all these years later I'm still convinced that this one experience came to me from a separate and inhuman force that lay outside my own mind and body. Though in my boyhood I'd certainly never read or heard of anything like it, my vision was of a kind experienced by more than a few lucky children and adults (it would be years before I knew that).

In brief, in a single full moment, I was allowed to see how intricately the vast contraption of nature all round me—and *nature* included me, my parents a few yards away in the house, all the animal life in the dense surroundings, and every other creature alive on Earth—was bound into a single vast ongoing wheel by one immense power that had willed us into being and intended our futures, wherever they might lead through the pattern, the enormous intricately woven pattern somehow bound at the rim and cohering for as long as the Creator willed it.

We were all, somehow, one vibrant thing; and even the bones of the vanquished Indians beneath my feet, the rattlesnakes I'd yet to encounter in the thickets but which I'd heard, the lethal microbes that had already invaded my body but spared me when I was an infant with whooping cough, and the plans of men like Adolf

Hitler—whom I'd heard of from my father (it was 1939 or '40)—were bound with the rest of us toward a final controlled harmony. At my age then, of course I couldn't have conceived a thing of such perfect complexity on my own; nor could I have described the gift I'd received in any such words. But memory tells me that the description is honest.

It's worth noting, more than sixty years later, that my vision took no specific account of the evil rampant in creation nor of contemporary cosmology's discovery that our universe seems bound on expanding, in a more and more rapid attenuation, toward the walls of space—if space has walls—though it seems to me now that, in my old vision, any given creature's duties to all other creatures were surely implicit in the grander image of one giant wheel of all created things.

So there that day, in the core of a childhood that was much-loved and cared for and that was generally happy though often unaccompanied, it seemed a useful revelation. It seems so still, unimpeachable in its eventual truth—an actual gift and not a deduction I made from the stories I'd heard and the human and animal life I'd observed. But it's worth remarking that the news reached me on one particular calendar day with no indication whatever that the Creator and impeller of such a harmony was best contemplated in some particular institution such as a church or on some especially holy day when he enjoined our worship in a church, a temple, or a mosque.

Did I think then, or do I believe later, that the vision was in any sense a direct call to me from God or some other intelligent force in nature? Was it a gesture uniquely intended to draw me near? Near to whom and for what? Am I ready to say, at this late point in my life, that I was singled out in childhood for special attention from God?

No, I'm not. I think it's possible that such revelations await a good many people who are lucky enough, or careful enough, to spend solitary time in feasible places and to be prepared—consciously or accidentally—to listen to a widely available transmission. I'd be lying if I didn't say that some part of my mind does sometimes feel that I was watched and called to, early in my life; but I don't guarantee it to anyone but myself.

And I surely can't have thought of a divine external source then. (Had I learned in Sunday school of God's call to the boy Samuel in the Hebrew First Book of Samuel, the third chapter?) The word *revelation* or the concept of a vision was unknown to me. Indeed the

---

◄ *Me in the woods adjacent to our house in Randolph County, North Carolina. Much of my fortunately solitary play was dedicated to restaging the stories of movies I'd seen—especially the Johnny Weissmuller Tarzan films, the Polynesian fantasies so popular in the '30s, starring Dorothy Lamour or Jon Hall, and anything to do with Native Americans. The time is the summer of 1939, very near—just before or after—my vision of the wheel of being that incorporates all nature, our own lives included.* (Courtesy of the author)

whole complex communication was far beyond a young boy's intelligence—so again, I'm all but compelled to assert that it not only came from a conscious source beyond my own mind but, further, that it came with a purpose.

Again, I think it's entirely possible that similar true glimpses await any human being—especially a child with an uncluttered mind—who can get sufficiently alone and quiet, which is one reason why, if I'd ever had children of my own, I'd have tried hard from the start to find a way to rear them outside any city—or at least in some place that gave the children frequent spells of calm and solitary time in the presence of uncluttered woods, streams, and relatively benign wild animals.

So while my experience didn't result in an immediate certainty that God knew me and tended me, it left me mildly watchful for the further intimations of which I'd heard. From early childhood, for instance, I'd been taught by my mother to say a common bedtime prayer that asked God to tend my sleep or, should I die in the night, to take me into his keeping. And I strongly suspect that my sudden vision of harmony—despite its lack of any directions or instructions—lay behind the increased interest I soon took in attending a nearby church and arranging for the baptism I'd yet to receive. Why?

In the world I knew then, and in the absence of other assigned sacred space, church was the main place which claimed to pay real respect to an unseen proprietor of things; and the nearest church happened to be Episcopalian (the denomination of my father's father—

my parents were Methodist and Baptist, a confusing family split that I was trying to paper over). Though North Carolina Episcopalians, known locally as "Whiskeypalians," were of the low-church persuasion in their rituals, their sanctuaries always had at least an altar with candles and colored hangings — an arrangement which made a visible gesture toward asserting that aesthetic beauty might be appropriate in the presence of God. That was a proposition which I'd heard from none of the other local and bleakly scoured Protestant churches of the upper South.

Another reality proved more enduring than the fact that I was tilted for a few years in the direction of church worship in a small Episcopal church that was only a short bike ride from our home. In a life that was still years away from puberty with its sexual awakening, my vision of absolute unity became my first crucial *private* knowledge, my first important secret. I never once mentioned what the vision had showed me, what I'd learned from it, not to my parents, my teachers, nor even to any of the few children I knew well enough to confide in. There were two of those, cousins my age who lived in close reach and with whom I shared a good deal but not my revelation. Absurd as it may sound for a boy of six or seven — and again I could not have defined it at the time — my life as a largely solitary mystic had begun.

I use the word *mystic* not in the current sense of one who employs exotic implements like crystals, flutes, or shaman rattles in his meditations or who performs self-designed rites in hopes of persuading the spirit world to illumine his present and supply his needs. When speaking of myself, I employ the words *mystic, mysticism, mystical* in the older sense of one whose relations with God are largely private and which follow no institutionally recommended and supervised path (the orthodox strands of Christianity, Judaism, and Islam have—understandably and often rightly—viewed their numerous mystics with suspicion if not persecution).

One reason I've always trusted the validity of my early back-yard vision is that I experienced no other such climactic moments in my childhood or for long years thereafter. I had many more happy days at play in the woods and elsewhere, yet I'm all but certain that I made no attempt whatever to bring on another such revelation (I did so as a summer-camp counselor in the Great Smoky Mountains a little more than ten years later; but the effort failed). The fact seemed to be that I'd seen it all—hadn't I?—in one fell childhood swoop. But was I old enough to realize even that much?

Four or five years later, I spent a memorable two summer weeks in an Episcopalian camp for boys in the North Carolina hills. We engaged in the usual hiking, swimming, softball playing, lanyard plaiting, and campfire singing. Those activities proceeded with a modest amount of Bible discussion and very few sessions of "church" but, again, with nothing whatever of a private spectacular nature. I had an active young imagination, to be sure—still fairly uncomplicated by the unrelenting hungers of adolescence—but I invented no visions for myself to rival the genuine thing that had come unbidden and so suddenly.

Still, my interest in Bible stories continued; and because at the age of nine I'd won a New Testament for bringing a new member to Sunday school, I soon began to read the Christian scriptures directly, not in the retellings of my earlier books nor in the short passages read out in church (had my parents been Jewish or Muslim or of some other faith, how different might my development have been?). The New Testament I'd won printed the actual words of Jesus in red ink, and that simple but powerful fact became important in the way I went. I could read long swatches of the red ink—Jesus' parables above all—and slowly I came to a deeply engaging sense of an actual man, one whom in general I could like, even if a sudden speech of his might leave me marooned in some activity which he deplored.

In time I'd come to read more and more of the connective black-ink passages; and with their provision of a credible narrative to contain the speeches, I began to construct an even more complex and arresting personality and character for Jesus—a man of great compassion, yes, and of towering wrath on occasion but also one of surprising wit and humor, of all things; and one who frequently contradicted himself, and did so with a healthy indifference to the fact that even surpasses Walt Whitman's startling

Do I contradict myself?
Very well then, I contradict myself,
(I am large, I contain multitudes.)

Above all, the four gospels—written in the first century and attributed only to the witnesses whom we call Matthew, Mark, Luke, and John—interested me with their varying but complementary pictures of a man as mysterious and potent yet riveting, eloquent, and credible as Jesus of Nazareth (an attentive reader quickly notes how much more arresting his own reported words are than those in the surrounding narrative passages written by the gospel writers themselves). For reasons I can't explain, neither my parents nor any other of my friends quite shared my fascination with the figure who emerged from my reading, and surprisingly few of my priestly and ministerial friends have done so in later years.

Given that from the age of five or six, I was also con-

◄ *In Jerusalem, the Dome of the Rock is a seventh-century shrine centered on a stone from which the Prophet Muhammad ascended into Heaven. That same stone is revered by Jews as the site of the altar or the Holy of Holies in the Temple built by King Solomon and rebuilt by Herod the Great. The Temple was destroyed in AD 70 by the Romans. Far below the Dome, Jews congregate for prayer alongside the enclosing Herodian wall that constitutes the only known remains of their Temple. Few images state so clearly the brutal contradictions frequently generated by religious faith.* (David H. Wells/Corbis)

sumed with a passion for painting and drawing, it's perhaps not odd that, by the time I was ten or eleven, Jesus was one of the figures I often thought about and tried to visualize. Above all then, I was greatly curious to know his actual physical appearance. Soon I was drawing frequent pictures of him—along with pictures of Tarzan and King Arthur, Alexander the Great, and Joan of Arc. Maybe I should add here that at no time in my early life did my contemporary school friends appear to think that I was in any sense weird. I made good grades and I seldom played sports, but nobody ever told me I was weird.

There was a growing difference though in my secret life. Almost from the start of my reading about Jesus, he seemed a focusing eye through which I could pass my early perception of the sole creating and organizing power of all nature. He was like the magnifying glass which I mostly used to examine the stamps I'd begun to collect. When I'd use the glass to pore over Hitler's face on a stamp, say, I could then take it out into the yard, capture a sunbeam, and soon have a thoroughly satisfying blaze under way in wood or paper scraps (like every survivor of boyhood I know, I'm a recovering pyromaniac).

By mid-adolescence my love of drawing had become the hope to be a painter in adult life, and I'd begun to collect books of old paintings. I was thus increasingly aware of the towering presence in Western art of Jesus at every stage of his brief, and brilliantly depictable, life. Among all the large figures in Western history, Jesus had the most arresting sense of how to create a memorable scene. Almost any one of his miracles, for instance, occurs at the core of a visually striking scene, as Rembrandt understood so convincingly and was gifted enough to portray in dozens of paintings and etchings.

In a way that may be difficult for you to imagine years from now, the preternaturally calm world around my childhood—indeed, most of small-town America in the 1930s and '40s—was as permeated with reverberations of the life of Jesus as the sea is with salt. And here at the start of the new millennium, with television on every side, he's still outrageously invoked as the guarantor of hatred, violence, and intolerant fantasy. In the middle-class world of my boyhood, a calmer and often weak-kneed Jesus prevailed in the churches. Perhaps in a uniformly racist world, our churches unconsciously chose to damp him down, to dilute the vehemence of his ethics (though, handily, he's never recorded as condemning the prevalent slavery of his culture). My parental families, incidentally, were far from Christ-haunted.

At that point in my life, I had no knowledge of the immense quantity of repression, torture, theft, and murder wreaked through past centuries—and still ongoing— in the name of Jesus by his self-proclaimed followers. For me the fact that the Jesus of the gospels was plainly a man who'd suffered and died for acts that appeared to be no more offensive than forgiveness, healing, and the claim to be a suffering messiah for the Jewish people made him more and more interesting as I began to encounter the sense of exclusion that often accompanies the approach of adolescence.

My rejection, like so many others, came at the hands of a pair of school bullies in a small town to which my family had moved when I was eleven — hardly a situation comparable to the final agonies of Jesus, as I was aware. Yet like many children who grow up in Christian cultures, then and perhaps even now, I spent a fair amount of secret time in prayer to Jesus, whom I had come to believe was a form of God himself. (When I say *believe* in such an instance, I hasten to add that I hardly possessed a trace of the theology that would have been required for an understanding of any such assertion. I'd been told that Jesus was God-on-Earth, and I'd come to feel it.)

In those urgent prayers, I'd ask for the bullies' meanness to stop and for kinder friends to materialize — my two demons had once seemed to be good friends but had turned violent against me, one afternoon in the midst of play, with no word of warning. And my prayerful request, repeated at least nightly for more than two years, was my first acquaintance with unanswered or partially answered prayer. Other friends appeared, along with fine schoolteachers, and their company was welcome. But my enemies never relented in the remaining two years till my parents moved us away from the poisoned town. Not that we moved because of my unhappiness; my parents had taken little note of it.

That only partial success with prayer didn't quite stop me. In fact, at the time it seemed no success at all. To this day, I have no idea of my enemies' motives, beyond sheer malice. But despite the silence from God, I'd begun to feel that even such a largely silent transaction might be the start of a dialogue that concerned itself with larger matters than upper-primate tribal hostility. Maybe in my first trial-run exposure to real pain, I'd cast God as a substitute for the friends who'd turned violent. I could address myself to him in the guaranteed ridiculous hope of hearing from my suddenly lost friends what Jesus promises in the Gospel of Matthew — "Come unto me all ye that labor, and are heavy laden, and I will give you rest."

In my futile pursuit of such an invitation from malicious human beings, life nonetheless slowly began to improve. In our new town, almost at once I had numerous likable acquaintances. On our block I promptly made a handful of friends, one or two of whom have lasted through my life; and at school I had numerous pleasant acquaintances and excellent demanding teachers. But almost anyone's adolescence, as you may know by the time you read this, is subject to attacks of self-doubt and melancholy — even bouts of dangerous despair.

Life can seem too pointless to continue; the world can seem blank-faced and unresponsive, if not unrelentingly malign. I never quite touched the full depths of self-revulsion, but there were still bleak stretches which I could communicate to no one because I couldn't imagine that anyone shared my failures of hope (though after nearly fifty years of teaching undergraduates, I can confidently assert that my experience was far from rare).

In my own case, that bleakness eventually began to flow from a bafflement that's likewise far from uncommon. Would I ever find the responsive love I longed for from another human? I was prepared to accept it from a boy, a girl, almost from a dog. Would the deep conviction of isolation that had, for years, lain behind my affable public self ever dissolve? Why should I ever have believed that things would change—and change for the better, as in fact things sometimes do—when like all young people I was essentially hopeless? You may remember that children are inclined to believe that the present situation, especially an unfavorable one, is unlikely to change. The prevalence of adolescent clinical depression and the daunting number of teenage suicides are predictable results of just such despair, and the prevailing religions of our culture seldom seem to reach such need.

Despite my own numerous hours of gazing at the ceiling in deep discouragement, I don't recall plunging toward the psychic trough where even a child may contemplate suicide; but still I went on investing a fair amount of time in prayers to Jesus and to his mother Mary. A beautiful Catholic girl in our neighborhood had taught me to recite the rosary, and it became a part of my attempts at reaching and persuading the Creator and—what?—his family to send permanent rescue.

The discovery of a woman's presence in the array of destinations for prayer proved a help that continues to this day (Protestantism has suffered badly from its late-medieval decision to eliminate a woman from its tar-

gets for prayer, especially since Jesus' mother—in the little we know about her—is mainly loyal and sympa-
thetic). Meanwhile, my otherwise kind parents seemed
unaware—as they'd been in our prior town—of my inter-
mittent hard times. Again, I think they rightly assumed
that children underwent the normal amount of human
pain; and perhaps wrongly, they made no special attempt
to combat mine (I shared one other great problem of
middle-class American children—I lacked any form of
psychically rewarding work and was thus left with a good
deal of idle moping-time on my hands).

So in the absence of my old tormentors, who'd even
made churchgoing difficult in our previous town, I
began attending church regularly—sometimes the
Methodist with Mother, sometimes the Baptist with
Dad. Independently of those Sunday observances, my
spiritual curiosities and allegiances intensified. That
may seem a strange development in the midst of a new
flood of happiness, but while I can't explain it (beyond
saying that perhaps I was growing a little more discern-
ing of the demands a responsible life placed upon me),
I can affirm its occurrence. And I began—for the first
time since my vision of the wheel—to feel like someone
who was sought. I felt, at the time, the danger of such a
conviction; and I've continued throughout my life to
remind myself that being sought by God, for his own
purposes, awards no human superiority. If anything, I felt
burdened.

Yet I'm still inclined to think that—by the age of fif-
teen—I was being approached again by a force that lay

well beyond myself, a force that was not human and that felt to me like what we call God. I should also repeat that I've never thought such approaches are rare on the part of God toward individual men, women, and children, though I think the approaches are often not recognized or are ignored. The chance that the needs of my own mind and body—stoked, as they were, in the fires of high puberty—were the fuel of those intensities no longer seems to me a serious possibility, despite the fact that Freudian psychiatry, and a good deal else, asserts that sexual hunger was surely at work.

In any case, the minister at my mother's church—a man of imposing dignity and eloquence—took a close interest in my developing curiosities about the historical Jesus and the origins of Christianity; and he readily agreed to what may have seemed a peculiar request from a growing boy. I asked him for joint prayer at what felt like critical points in my life and for private communion at times when I felt the need of special help, times such as college scholarship competitions; and he readily agreed.

It didn't then seem inappropriate to me to approach the Creator of the universe with personal concerns that risked triviality if not absurdity. If God had made me, I thought—and made my private needs feel so urgent—then he would at least be available to listen. Or so at least Jesus had claimed more than once in the gospels, especially when he says "Ask and it shall be given" or when he assures us that "Even the hairs of your head are numbered."

By age seventeen I clearly had some tendency toward a life that would make regular attempts to bring God's attention to bear on my better aims and to seek his cooperation in them. Did I feel by then what I hadn't felt in the wake of my early vision of the great wheel of being—that I'd been, as the saying was, *called* toward a lifetime's career as a full-time religious person, an ordained minister? No, I never did and I'm all but sure that neither my parents nor my minister ever suggested it. For a good while in fact, I'd taken pains to conceal my religious concerns from most of my kin and friends.

Apart from normal adolescent hijinks, I didn't behave in contradictory ways; but it was both a function of my innate character, and a conscious form of harmless concealment, that my daily behavior by no means looked unusually "holy." In fact, I was a steady clown in a good many of my high-school activities, despite the fact that my editorials for the school newspaper had the familiar organ sound of youthful self-importance.

If I'd even glanced at such a career, as a Southern Protestant I'd have seen that the possibilities were limited to the pulpit ministry and the organ or choir loft. The thought of teaching religion in a seminary or university would not then have occurred to me; and though I'd studied piano since the age of ten, and was acquiring a large collection of classical and popular records, I had no expert musical skills nor any intention of acquiring them. Only the pulpit ministry would have lain before me then; and toward the end of high school, an especially influential teacher suggested that I think of preparing for life as a pastor.

Though by then I'd joined the Methodist church and attended regular services, I felt at once that her suggestion was wrong. My sexual energies seemed far too powerful and, by then, heretical for such a career. I was also beginning to feel an abiding distrust of a trait that has long been a danger in all the religions I've observed—the tendency on the part of individual church members to pour adulation on a locally stellar minister who's then mightily tempted to preen in the constant bath of praise.

Luckily, I'd already decided on the parallel careers I've ultimately followed—life as a writer and a teacher. My teacher had likewise encouraged me powerfully in those aims, and she seemed content with my choice. Moving on to college then, I headed in those directions. As I worked at my undergraduate studies (which included an important course in the history of the Hebrew and Greek Bible) and, privately, on my writing (especially poetry)—and as I began to express my sexual needs—I also began to feel less comfortable in receiving the praise I'd enjoyed for the past few years in my church. I was not the good boy whom many people thought me.

I'd even begun to suspect that an unadmirable appetite for display was part of much formal worship; and that seemed true not merely for the minister but for many public worshipers, including me. I felt that I'd begun to value, far too much, the way I thought I *looked* in the eyes of my fellow worshipers. Yet despite my involvement in several university courses that questioned — and occasionally mocked — the foundations of religious thought, my gradual withdrawal from participation in any church community represented no loss of the faith that had grown as I grew.

Withdrawal was likewise a response to my increasing awareness of the hostility or indifference of almost all American Christian churches — and not only in my native South — to the coming crises in racial justice and in the understanding of any forms of the adult expression of love other than those specifically licensed in Hebrew and Christian scripture (I'd already noticed how few things Jesus has to say about sex, how he condemns almost none of it except whoremongering and any harm to children).

In most moral concerns, congregations are at least 90 percent dependent on the guidance of their minister; and it's a mere fact that I graduated from both high school and Duke University without hearing so much as a word of attempted comprehension of sexual complexity. Above all, for me then — and truly incredibly for one who was reared in the South — I'd heard no syllable from any white minister who condemned, or even mentioned, American racism. (When some ministers began to show more courage a few years later, many of them discovered how quickly they could be dismissed from their segregated churches for defying the will of congregations who gave few signs of having read the gospels.)

Honestly, though, I think that my own withdrawal was an answer to an even earlier claim on my deepest instincts in the matter. It was a return to the means of worship that had long been more natural and useful for me — a worship that had begun when I began my roaming of our neighboring woods, even before my vision of the great wheel. After the vision — as I've tried to make clear above — my spiritual exercises had gradually come to consist of private prayer, reading, meditation, and my eventual beginnings of an understanding that the chief aims of any mature religious life are union with the will of God, as opposed to one's own will, and the finding of ways to assist other creatures on their own lonely routes. The fact that I've frequently failed in both aims is a matter for a further look below.

My first year of graduate study in England, where such study is largely self-guided, marked also my launching on a serious dedication to my writing and on my first real delight in reciprocated love, with all its complications. In the chilly atmospheres of the oldest college at Oxford and its magnificently stark fourteenth-century chapel whose pale gray emptiness echoed the rapid shrinkage (in the mid twentieth century) of Protestant Anglicanism in Britain, it was easy enough to avoid any search for a congenial church. And my sense of the Creator — of the duties I owed him and his creatures and the means of communicating with him — continued on the solitary track to which they'd begun to revert before I left home for three years abroad. Yet in fairly normal human fashion, I was now praying chiefly when I needed quick help (the adolescent mystic was drying up remarkably).

I felt brief mild guilt at my separation from a religious community, especially when my mother or my old minister wrote to inquire about my British churchgoing; but I told myself I'd made a necessary choice, for the time at least. I imagined that I'd eventually learn to find, through my teaching and writing, communities where my own questions and useful findings could best be exercised and conveyed to others. I thought I could find a wider community than I might find in a dedicated building and an enclosed congregation which might return me to the self-regard I regretted from my past experiences.

Meanwhile, as that separation continued, a curious paradox grew. As I traveled through England and Italy, the Saxon and Norman village churches, the Gothic cathedrals, and the Baroque basilicas and churches I visited became what felt like real replacements for the worship services I'd left at home. The huge structures themselves—Canterbury, Ely, York Minster, Durham, and Wells in England; the Milan cathedral, the Sistine Chapel, St. Peter's itself, and Santa Maria Maggiore (the final three in Rome)—were plainly great webs flung out by generations of builders, sculptors, painters, and stained-glass makers in the hope of netting as much of the Spirit as will pause for human contemplation. And there, on my own, I confirmed again my bent toward private worship (empty churches, sometimes filled with

unexpected music, worked far better for me than crowded ones; and the bent continues still).

In long retrospect I estimate that my subsequent years of work as a writer and teacher may have communicated—to a few hundred thousand readers and a few thousand students—the way in which one relatively lucid and respectably educated man has managed to live at least six decades of a life that (while it's committed a heavy share of self-intoxicated incursions on others and has broken at least five of the Ten Commandments) has so far hurled no dead bodies to the roadside. I've likewise abandoned no sworn partners or children, and have managed to turn up—shaved and sober—in a writing office, a teaching classroom, a kinsman's or lover's or friend's place of need on most promised occasions. My students can learn at least that much from campus rumor, occasional remarks of mine in class, or my published work.

I've been especially chary of broaching anything resembling full discussions of my private relations with

---

◀ *Wells Cathedral, a thirteenth-century structure in the small town of Wells, England. The three striking inverted arches at the crossing which surrounds the altar were added in the fourteenth century when lower supports proved insufficient to bear the weight of the tower above. The resulting effect of the repair is entirely original, mysteriously startling, and an ultimate witness to human fallibility and resourcefulness.* (Angelo Hornak/ Corbis)

God in the arenas of either of my careers, in writing or in university classrooms. I don't see my secular classrooms as pulpits. So for years at Duke I've taught Milton's *Paradise Lost*, the most deeply probing religious text in our language, and the Gospels of Mark and John; but I do so with almost no discussion of my own beliefs. That's partly because, by nature, I'm among the world's least proselytizing souls but also because the particular shape of my beliefs formed itself so gradually, and in response to such personal tides, as to be almost incommunicable if not incomprehensible to others.

In recent years, however, I've relaxed a little on the subject if they come to me in private. But I still decline to *talk* about my private religious experience with most individuals and with all groups. And that reluctance is almost entirely owing to my realization that impromptu speech, in my case at least, is prone to headlong imprecision which I'm eager to avoid. Writing about faith, though, has become a different matter for me — one more subject to scrupulous and exact expression.

I've written of my faith in two volumes of memoir, a number of poems, a published letter to a dying young man who asked for my views, a study of the ethics of Jesus; and now I'm writing this new letter to you. Even at Duke University, after more than thirty years of teaching *Paradise Lost*, I've begun very lightly to confess to my students that I'm a renegade Christian and that they might be at a certain advantage in studying a Christian poet such as Milton with me. Wouldn't they like to study Homer with, say, an actual Zeusian or ancient Persian poetry with a Zoroastrian (might it be devastating, though, to study Christianity with an actual first-century Galilean disciple of Jesus or Judaism with one of the younger sons of the patriarch Jacob; might such men or women seem repellent to us now, and might they find our faith bizarrely inaccurate)?

In my fiction I've yet to be as overtly religious as older contemporaries like Graham Greene, Evelyn Waugh, Muriel Spark, and Walker Percy; and I still can't imagine going as far as they in a novel. No other American novelist or poet of my generation appears to have done so either. My own reluctance is largely a function of my renegade relation to formal Christianity—I'm especially loath to risk driving off non-Christian readers with even the faintest whiff of incense. I'm keenly aware of how otherwise intelligent Americans are inclined to dismiss any form of religious writing or talk, especially on the subjects of Jesus and Christianity—two realities which continue to spawn the most offensive strands of such communication—so I've tried to write fiction which is true to my own mind without spooking others.

But the moral values that Christianity shares with most other religions run steadily beneath my work as ideal traits of human life—those values and an implicit praise of the always startling degree of tolerance and compassion shown and commended by Jesus. I say *startling* because I'm always caught off guard by that characteristic whenever I read about him. Is there, in all of history, an earlier human being who displays those degrees of goodness, not to speak of the most ignored of all his commands (that we refrain from all violence, even a defensive response to another's violence)? Though the first three gospels report stern warnings and occasional condemnations from him, when he examines human behavior in the abstract, it's the literal truth that nowhere in any of the four gospels does he repel a single person or group who approaches him honestly and without hostility. No one would be more appalled than he by the intolerance and hatred, frequently amounting to psychic violence, that pour from so many present sects which parade under his name.

Perhaps another sign of faith that's visible in my work is the fact that almost none of the many dozen characters in my novels and plays is an atheist (so far as we know their full history), though most of them fail in their ethics if not their morals. It's a notorious fact that a thoroughly good character, in fiction at least, is almost always an incredible or boring character or both. In my poetry, faith does sporadically come to the fore; but some form of poetry has always been the prime vehicle of all faiths and must surely continue to be so—as indeed, alongside music, it's one of our two chief modes of artistic beauty.

(And is there a modern culture that agrees to call *beautiful* any poem—or song or story for that matter—which recommends or extols human behavior which that culture calls *evil*? I suspect the answer is no. Why are there, for a single instance, no surviving Nazi poems which a majority of us can call *beautiful*; why are there no widely compelling songs from the Ku Klux Klan, no enduring narratives or films which send us into the streets with "Cry havoc" in our throats along with a craving for blood? And is that why Keats's Grecian urn can say to the poet, at the end of his great ode, "Beauty is truth, truth beauty"?)

So—patient friend—my life went on through youth and middle age. It was subject, as I've said, to real wrongdoing. A detailed catalog of my failures, here and now, would likely be of no help to you. When you begin to accumulate sins of your own, you'll know what they are (they are not especially exotic); and I hope you'll have the beginnings, at least, of a sense of how to deal with them—how to stop them in their tracks before they can hurt anyone but yourself. To speak of one wrong that I can discuss freely here, I'm especially troubled as I age by the fact that, while I've tried regularly to share my good income, I've mostly failed, largely ignoring the devastating needs of the wretched and homeless near at hand, not to speak of a wider world. And while I don't raise the point to deflect guilt from myself, I'll have to remark that nothing seems to me more baffling in most religious institutions than the prosperity of so many self-declared Christians (and Jews and Muslims and Buddhists, so far as I can see) and their ministers.

Few aspects of Jesus' teaching are more concealed in sermons by modern Christian ministers, but any clear-eyed reading of the gospels makes it undeniable that Jesus condemned wealth throughout his career. Even his rough-hewn head disciple, the fisherman Peter, hears Jesus say that "It's easier for a camel to go through a needle's eye than for a rich man to enter Heaven." The fisherman responds angrily "Look, we gave up everything and followed you." Peter means presumably that he and at least some of the other disciples have followed Jesus in the hope of the sort of prosperity that the followers of so many contemporary ministers have acquired by their loyalty—good food, clothes, and houses. We can only imagine Jesus' bitter smile in Peter's direction. And don't let anyone tell you that the needle's eye of which Jesus speaks was some particular narrow gate in a city wall—there was apparently no such gate. Jesus may have been engaging in hyperbole; he was also dead earnest. So again, in the matter of sufficient help to the poor and other needy, I include myself in a list of the delinquent. While I'm far from the richest man I know, I think I have more than I need, though my paraplegic old age is consuming more than I ever thought I'd require.

In my first five decades, I was frequently challenged by disappointment in my life and work and by at least one pervading remorse. Throughout those adult decades—despite several deep dives into self-blame and the lack of any clear view ahead in various departments of life—my faith has been a prime stabilizer and guide. But like many other navigational aids that save us in straits, both minor and desperate, faith has done most of its work when I had only the dimmest awareness of its service to me. In short, I've been a man who seeks God most assiduously when I'm forced by personal folly or by fate to scramble in the hope of digging myself a trench against incoming fire. God, meanwhile, has seen to my safety and my working endurance when I mainly dodged my duties to him.

Then when I was fifty-one, in a few quick weeks, I found myself undergoing increasing difficulties in walking with my usual ease and steadiness. After a good deal of whistling-in-the-dark denial, I went to my doctor and was found to have a long and intricately entangled cancer within my spinal cord. Despite surgery, with the best technology of the early 1980s and at the hands of a brilliant and humane surgeon, very little of the tumor's mass could be removed; and no effective neural chemotherapy was then available.

The only medical hope was five weeks of searing radiation, directly to the fragile cord itself. I was warned, by a radiation oncologist of baffling frigidity, that such a brutal therapy might leave me paraplegic or worse. The alternative was to wait while the tumor paralyzed my legs, then my arms and hands, and finally my lungs. With no other proffered choice, I agreed to the radiation, perhaps wrongly.

A few mornings before the daily treatments were to start, I was propped wide awake in bed at home when I experienced the second visionary moment of my life, some forty-five years after my childhood glimpse of the unity of all being. I've written at length about this second moment in other places. It's enough to say here that I was half-upright in my bed; then suddenly without apparent transport—and I was certainly not dreaming—I was lying on the stony shore of a huge lake. I knew at once

that I was by the Sea of Galilee (Lake Kinnereth, as it's called in modern Israel)—and in a moment, a man whom I knew to be Jesus had silently beckoned me into the water with him.

In another moment—still silent—he was washing the foot-long wound from the failed surgery that had gouged for hours deep into my spinal cord; that wound was also the proposed site of my weeks of radiation. At last Jesus spoke, only a four-word sentence—"Your sins are forgiven." But nearly overwhelmed as I'd been by a month of surgery and the discouraging aftermath, I pushed him onward for the answer I most wanted—"Am I also healed?" As if I'd forced it from him, he said only "That too." And though he gave no obvious sign of anger at my question, he said nothing more and waded back to land, through the water ahead of me. The experience ended there as inexplicably as it came. It had been nonetheless a long moment as vivid as any other in my life—and as undeniable in its force.

My conviction, more than twenty years after that

◄ *This drawing was made by me in the summer of 1984, shortly after my vision of healing in the waters of Lake Kinnereth—the Sea of Galilee. It records, as nearly as I could then manage, an actual visionary event that I both watched and participated in—Jesus pouring lake water down the long scar which remained from my initial failed cancer surgery. The scar is boxed by the gentian purple dye that marks it for the withering radiation I'll soon receive.* (Courtesy of the author)

second vision, is that the experience was in some crucial sense real. In a human action that apparently lasted no longer than two minutes, I was essentially healed. By *healed* I mean that I was repaired in the sense that a man I had every reason to trust had guaranteed me a long stretch of ongoing vigorous existence. The fact that my legs were subsequently paralyzed by twenty-five X-ray treatments—two years before a new device made the removal of the tumor possible—was a mere complexity in the ongoing narrative which God intended me to make of my life.

Or did I err in agreeing to the radiation? When I published an earlier account of the morning in Lake Kinnereth, a woman in Mexico wrote and asked me why I persisted with the chancy radiation when I'd already been healed. She hinted that my faith had failed me at a crucial point. I occasionally wonder still. There does seem at least a possibility that, had I at once accepted the import of such a convincing vision and declined the withering radiation, I might not have suffered the entire paralysis of my lower body.

My doctors felt that, along with its damage, the radiation had nonetheless stalled the tumor for a lucky two years till an appropriate surgical tool was perfected. I'm more inclined than not to agree with them; but it's unlikely I'll ever know (and did Jesus' almost dismissive words "That too" imply that he'd healed me in my own terms, that I was freed by his washing to live as I wished, not as I'd formerly lived?).

I'm aware that many of my contemporaries, and virtually all my doctors, will read such a statement as groundless if not howling crazy. I can come near to sharing their laughter. Yet more than two decades after my initial all-but-hopeless diagnosis, I'm still an energetic working man when virtually none of my initial therapists appeared to think I had a real chance for substantial survival. At the start of my trouble in 1984, one of them told my brother that I had eighteen more months of life at best. And at the end of the radiation, when I was at my absolute lowest ebb of vitality with severe burns on my upper back and neck, I asked my kindly neurosurgeon if I needed "to start making plans," meaning of course "plans to die." He didn't smile and say "Of course not." He said "I'll tell you when you do."

Well, by then—for nearly two months—I'd been effectively healed, as I increasingly came to believe. And I've never doubted that my survival came with large help from my surgeon and abiding care from God. You can likely imagine that my relations with God reached a record of lifetime intensity in the summer of my first surgery and for the three years of recovery and adjustment to grinding pain (which has never relented, not for a single waking hour of two decades). I hung on, as successfully as I could—which was not always—to the promise of my vision. My failures of trust in the Kinnereth moment, however, never invaded my prayer life. While I sometimes felt I was bound to die soon, I never accused God of bad faith with me nor felt that death would be appalling, though I prayed to live if life was his will for me.

And since, as I told you, I mentioned my healing elsewhere, I've had many letters from patently sane strangers who confide similar, though very individual, transcendent experiences in times of dire trouble. They mostly describe a waking experience in which some entirely real and palpable figure—whether the man Jesus or another matter-of-fact plainclothes visitor—comes and consoles them in an agonized time or heals them of a grave illness. Such confidences almost always end with my correspondents telling me that they'd never previously revealed their experience to anyone else for fear of ridicule.

They almost always say also that their experience, like mine, was singular. That is, the inexplicable visit had never been repeated, thereby apparently eliminating the possibility that we'd all been merely cheering ourselves with pleasant delusions in the face of calamity. I can't speak for my correspondents; but surely—if I'd invented my healing in Kinnereth or only dreamt it—my own near-desperate need for encouragement in the next two years of increasing paralysis (plus a broken back resulting from a fall, three further surgeries, and the remorseless pain that accompanies most serious damage to the central nervous system) might have made a mind as narrative-prone as mine invent further helpful scenes to guide me forward in dreams or visions.

Yet my moment in Lake Kinnereth has not recurred

in any form in my life. If he could be asked now, the laconic Jesus of my one encounter might well say "Why should it need to happen again?" (there's only one, quite amusing, reported moment in the gospels, as he heals the blind man in Bethsaida, when Jesus must try a second time before the cure succeeds). Those years have brought me an unprecedented amount of work — twenty-five books since the cancer — and an outpouring of affection and meticulous care of a sort I wouldn't have allowed myself to expect from kin, friends, and strangers. In addition to the books, I've continued my regular schedule of teaching — one semester each year.

I've traveled for business and for pleasure even more than in my able-bodied life. I won't say that my seated life has been consistently happier than the five decades that preceded it. I will say, though, that those profound changes have deepened my conviction that the illness — its devastations and its legacies of paralysis and pain — was intended for me, both when it arrived so suddenly and perhaps ever after. My doctors felt that, like many spinal cancers, mine was perhaps congenital — my companion from the womb till at least the age of fifty-six.

In the presence of such a reality, many sane men and women — now and in earlier centuries — have asserted that they find it impossible either to believe in or to worship a deity who would actively will one of his creatures to suffer without an announced, or at least an apparent, reason. The banner bearer for such sentiments in modern literature is Dostoevsky's Ivan Karamazov, who declares that he cannot bow to a God who wills, or permits, the suffering of a single innocent child.

As well as almost anyone alive, I can understand the strength of such contentions, the agonized fury involved in them—especially in the case of parents who've watched, or are watching, a tormented child—but I can also point to a central weakness in the still-considerable power of such objections. Despite an initial emotional eloquence, aren't they finally as lacking in substance as my saying, for instance, that I could not respect a whale which—for unfathomable reasons—attacked and destroyed a whaling ship with its crew aboard? I grant that the comparison—despite its origin in the history of nineteenth-century whaling—is seriously flawed since the whale did not create the ship and its crew (and so far as I know, only some groups of the Inuit people currently worship or attach supernal significance to whales); but bear with me for these questions at least.

How, precisely, does my announced failure of respect for the whale affect it in the slightest? And doesn't my announcement render me merely absurd (as it does Ivan Karamazov, likable as he is in some other ways)? In the minds of those drowning seamen, the giant marauder must have seemed malign in its anger if not its purpose. They—and I—will never comprehend the whale's intent any more than I can understand my presumed God's intent in crippling and tormenting me, if indeed his will was at work in the matter. In early childhood, for one example, I suffered sporadic and mysterious seizures that subsided only as I neared school age. I can remember a few of them; but I recall no related pain, though I could see that my parents were terrified as they struggled to cool my sudden spike of intense fever.

To attempt to go deeper is a far more daunting plunge—to plumb, say, the mind of a God who may simply observe, without healing (if he can, which I assume he can), the tortured death of a child from cancer or the murder of millions of children and adults by mad statesmen and their henchmen. It would also be a plunge which shows the diver a vast sweep of terrible and imponderable sights through the backward reaches of history, not to speak of the dreadful present.

Yet such an investigation remains a journey that doesn't leave me, or most other believers (and few of us appear to be psychotic masochists), with a need to refuse God's request for worship and to deny our own need of his help. If a God exists and if that God desires worshipful respect from us—as the Gods of Judaism, Christianity, Islam, theistic Buddhism, and Hinduism say that they do—then my personal ethical conclusions about my God's behavior are ludicrously irrelevant to the nature of things and may well cloud my reputation as a creature from whom intelligence may well be expected.

Meanwhile for me, through nearly a third of my life, I've barely attempted to guess what the main intention may be of such a blow as my own paralysis and continued pain. Fragmentary guesses would include the thought that I was meant to do my work more steadily and better than I'd previously managed or that I was meant to become a better creature in my relations with other creatures. Time, or any space that may be available beyond time, will presumably uncover as much of that mystery as I'll ever need to know (note that I'm hardly languishing in hot curiosity, even now). I can say, however, without supplying the Polaroids from my old bedroom, that the drastic reversal in my life—its severe and worsening physical damages—led me to near-abandonment of the sexuality that I'd always explored with pleasure, the enduring rewards of love and loyalty, pain and remorse.

I'm one of the least puritanical souls presently alive on the planet, but I've made that simplification in my daily life because I slowly came to suspect that a transformation of one of my past modes of love may have been among the intentions of the externally catastrophic change in my life. And while this new course has left me deprived of a few much-prized rewards, in the face of new gains, I've all but ceased to miss them. If nothing else, paraplegia either leads to a rapid fining-down of one's focus—and one's expectations from other creatures—or it plunges its cripple into querulous, or wailing, neurosis or worse: certainly a creature whom no one else wants to know.

Yet now I've outlived both my parents (Dad died at fifty-four, Mother at sixty); and though I'm past seventy, I'm hopeful of as much more time as I have work to do, the resources with which to do it, and the steady help I need in my straitened circumstances. My present relations with God run the fairly tranquil course which I take to be common to many believers. As I've mentioned, those relations intensify when I'm in trouble. When the turbulence calms, they tend to resemble the domestic relations of the members of a family—a good deal of taking-for-granted on my part, with a dozen or so snatches of prayer per day—*Please help me do so and so, please guard me from such and such, help me be a better man here.* Some others are brief requests to understand God's intent, if any; to learn patience, to bear what I can't change, and then to incorporate it into my ongoing days.

I'm not yet profoundly troubled with fears of age or death, though as an unmarried and unchilded man, I can see that such worries may lie ahead. As a cripple I'm also steadily troubled by the search for constant live-in help. Yet I have no doubt that the usual quiet in which I exist—and here I tap on the nearest available wood—comes as a form of mercy from the force that created the world and knows of me in it. Nonetheless I'm aware my great luck could change at any moment. It's happened before and while I won't say I'm ready for further changes, I reckon I'm a little more hardened than some.

Can I expect that such a spotty run through seven decades of your old friend's faith will have any useful weight for you, years from now, or for anyone else to whom religious belief is a baffling phenomenon, an inviting curiosity, or an intellectually impossible position? From a friend like you, I might hope for the endurance required to read these pages—a little more than two hours, say. And maybe something in our friendship, which began in your early childhood, will lend these words the force that words from a longtime friend or kinsman may have when all others fail.

I can hardly expect this compact story, long as it may have seemed, to be convincing for unbelieving strangers, though I can still hope it may detain a thoughtful few. And I'm all but sure I can do nothing more about that, not here and now—unless some unpredictable wind of good fortune carries these pages into far more hands than I might now expect. If a welcome few make the attempt to hear me out and then feel trapped in a monomaniacal aria, I trust that they'll exit promptly, running.

Faced with the hope of feeding your adult curiosities, I have nothing more authentic to offer by way of commending faith to a young man or woman. But I'd guess that the lives of a few great believers might. You could do worse than to start with Augustine, say, in his monumental *Confessions* and the life and example of Francis of Assisi as recorded by his colleagues in *The Little Flowers of St. Francis.* The remarkably winning Francis left behind no lengthy biographical or theological writing of his own, but his brief life is as potent an argument as I know of for the selfless benefits of belief. His ultimate extreme suffering is an apparent result of his saintliness (he's the first person on record to bear the stigmata). And the fact that a creature as charitable as Francis should suffer is further evidence that God, in so many religions, seems compelled to teach human beings largely through pain (is it because of our recalcitrance, as a species?). And while *The Little Flowers* is marked by a medieval sheen of fancy that may occasionally need to be polished away, it's the earliest still-useful sustained account of an instructive good man's life and work.

Yet despite the labor of numerous capacious minds, we live in a time when faith apparently can almost never be imparted by rational persuasion—could it ever?—though Christianity continues to stand high among major religions in its ancient and ongoing attempt to convert the unbelieving. Only Islam now tries as hard or harder. Given the difficulty of deriving faith from one's reading, I can add that one of the often repellant requirements for acquiring faith in adult life is the generally unacknowledged necessity that faith be given advance help from God. The most sophisticated theologies of the Western past—millennia of rabbinical debate and the treatises of Augustine, Aquinas, Calvin, Kierkegaard, and Barth, among others—deduce a similar necessity.

The leap of faith that believers so often recommend to their baffled friends is preceded by an immensely serious hitch; for the leap almost invariably demands God's presence, on the far side of the abyss, saying "*Jump!*" In Christianity anyhow, strict Calvinists fervently agree. They assert that God has decided, from the beginning of time, that he'll call certain creatures to believe in him and thus to win salvation. Others he simply permits, for his own never-disclosed reasons, to live and die in pre-ordained damnation. It's another idea that looks absurd to anyone who has not been inclined to faith by a propitious early atmosphere and training, and the possibility

is attractive to no one but the hateful. Yet all major religions accord God the right to make his own choices, despite the refusal of Ivan Karamazov.

For me, as for more than one writer of the early Christian documents comprised in the New Testament, that terrible prior choosing by God seems at times the baldest deduction from attentive witness of the world (a great part of the American population from the seventeenth through at least the nineteenth centuries lived in horrified confrontation with the likelihood of damnation, and few beliefs can have caused more suicides). And still indeed, some lives flourish; some wither quite inexplicably—unless you believe in predestination. I'm not saying that such a daunting conclusion lies at the core of my own belief. But I am saying, again, that close observation of the human race throughout world history may well produce such a faith in the thoughtful observer. If I shared such a bleak faith, I'd hardly be attempting to persuade you onward now.

◄ *Bernini's tall bronze seventeenth-century canopy rises above the high altar of St. Peter's Basilica in Rome. The altar itself stands—according to ancient tradition, which may have been confirmed in the twentieth century—over the tomb of Jesus' chief disciple, the fisherman Peter. That so much grandeur confronts us in a church built to celebrate the divinity of a dirt-poor carpenter and itinerant rabbi from the first-century Galilean village of Nazareth, in the Roman province of Palestine, is another of the enigmas of the world's prevailing religion.* (Giansanti Gianni/Corbis Sygma)

How can anyone reared in the desert air of so much contemporary science—and physics seems the science most relevant to religious questions—begin to move in the murky directions of faith, especially when so many manifestations of religious belief (Christian, Muslim, Jewish, and Hindu) often lead to violence, disdain if not outright hatred for other humans, and dithering or murderous nonsense? In any day's news, half the world's wrongs seem committed in the name of some god. That one obstacle to faith, if no other, is all but impassably high. Yet again, the majority of human beings claim some form of faith (it would be easy enough to speculate that born-violent men and women are attracted to religion).

It's my seasoned instinct, then, that any slow scrutiny of contemporary science will demonstrate at many points its intellectual inadequacy as an ample chain of theories to explain the entire face and actions of the world. (This is not to endorse the presently developing doctrine of intelligent design. If there was an intervention by God in our evolution, it was inevitably far more preliminary and far more mysterious than anyone has yet come near to comprehending—or may ever. Such an untrackable intervention is not beyond my notion of a God who, so often, displays—among his infinite clash of characteristics—a tendency to comedy.) American medical science and especially its daily practice on the living, for instance—which might prove especially illuminating— is among the most intellectually and emotionally parched of disciplines, as I've learned at first hand. But the situation was not always so.

Isaac Newton, who in many ways invented what we call science, was a believer (if a rather mad-sounding one) as was Gottfried Wilhelm Leibniz, who asked one of the ultimate questions — "Why is there something and not nothing?" That's a question which, to me, seems challenging enough to justify the start of any number of divine investigations. William James called it "the darkest question in all philosophy." Though the various departments of science have illuminated many realities since those men worked in the early modern era, it has found almost nothing to assail any thoughtful faith in a Creator. Certainly nothing in Darwinian evolution, even in its most contemporary forms, seriously assails the reality of God. And there are presently intriguing signs that, the further quantum physics proceeds in our own time, the more nearly its discoveries resemble a new branch of theology.

Here at the beginning of the third millennium, physics is uncovering at an astonishing rate subatomic phenomena that surpass the imaginings of the wildest hierophant scraping his sores with a cast-off potsherd — phenomena which resemble nothing so much as a combination of very high and very low comedy: Shakespearean-style reconciliation and Chaplinesque farce as minute particles of matter elude one another over gigantic distances yet communicate with exquisite unanimity, then reconnect in an instant with a possible joy (have I lured you into subatomic physics?—phone me collect if you begin to understand it).

That's not to claim that anyone should fling posthaste into the arms of a dancing configuration of material particles or kneel at the feet of any new form of God which those particles might imply or any religious sect simply because, for the past two centuries, science has proven so prissily bankrupt as a guide to what's here and what's there (in quantum physics our concepts of *here* and *there* seem increasingly to be the same thing). Quite enough helium-filled New Age unfortunates are steadily nattering away on television to warn us off any precipitous fling into such current cant terms as "spiritual values" or "spiritual awareness." Yet if nothing else, an honest well-informed creature must now acknowledge that the world—the universe of physical objects, forces, and actions above, within, or below the range of human or instrumental vision—far surpasses in extent and wonder, and perhaps in mystery, any reality that we can see and absorb, even with our newly superb and rocket-launched telescopes and monitoring systems.

But if anyone with a persistent curiosity about faith, anyone who has lacked a sane early grounding in one of the central faiths of his or her culture, were to ask me where to go to begin to understand the inevitability of belief and its mixed rewards (faith is more difficult than unbelief), I'd suggest two initial courses, each to be pursued with quiet steadiness. First, begin to read the sacred texts of your native culture. Given your family origins, Harper, those would be the Hebrew and Christian texts comprised in the Bible. Choose relatively new translations and move slowly enough so that you don't give up quickly from sheer indigestion. Those documents don't always make for easy reading, especially in the lengthy legal codes and genealogies and the fulminations of some of the prime Old Testament prophets, who can sometimes seem less relevant than the chattering of birds.

Persist, though, and I trust you'll begin to feel drawn in by the Bible's broad narrative arcs. The long history of Israel and the brief career of Jesus (perhaps no more than a year) and, later, the driven efforts of his followers (convinced as they are of his resurrection) are the greatest stories we possess. Hebrew scripture—in its earliest oral form and its later written texts—may well have emerged through more than a thousand years and was set down, by various writers, almost entirely in evolving stages of the Hebrew language.

The Christian scriptures are virtually all products of the first-century world of imperial Rome and are written in that form of Greek which was then the common language of the Mediterranean basin, the most lasting gift of Alexander the Great in the wake of his victorious march through the known world of his time. So the Bible alone, however daunting in a thousand ways, can offer you numerous worlds of thought about God, ranging from the hot erotic verse of the Song of Solomon through the terrible and finally unanswerable examination of God's justice in the Book of Job and on into the magnanimous life and healing career of Jesus with its steady insis-

tence on the unfailing love of God for each human being.

At that point, I often feel the rising of my only severe questions of Jesus, whose desolate dying words from the cross in the Gospels of Mark and Matthew are "My God, my God, why did you forsake me?" How I'd like to ask the risen Jesus for a final expansion on that awful question. The actual words are a quotation from the opening of Psalm 22, a long Hebrew poem which ends more hopefully than it begins; but surely it's near impossible to believe that a man nailed by hands and feet to an upright cross is reciting ancient poetry as a means of cheering himself.

The Gospels of Luke and John give him quite different last words, perhaps in an effort to make his final conscious moments appear less desperate. But Matthew and Mark, the oldest gospel, face up to an awful question. Did Jesus' own ghastly suffering alter his understanding of God's nature? Is God's love invariably unfailing after all—and unfailing for something as

---

◄ *Despite the fact that the great galaxy in Andromeda is the nearest galaxy to our own (the Milky Way), its light takes nearly three million years to reach us. Many astronomers speculate that a black hole lies at the center of this galaxy, like many others, and is consuming the galaxy ferociously. This early photograph was taken at the Jervissy Observatory in France.* (Bettmann/Corbis)

minuscule in all creation as a single human being? Can God even, in any meaningful sense, be said to love our entire galaxy—a minor wheel of stars and gasses among uncountable other such wheels in perhaps uncountable other universes?

If so, why can so few of us consistently believe such a claim, especially at the most difficult moments of our lives? Why does God so often seem to have vanished, or to stand aside in unreachable silence, in our most frightening and painful times? If you advance at least some distance into belief, you'll of course have your own questions; and some of them will find no answers. But many transcendent realities around us, from the Grand Canyon to a Vermeer painting, decline to answer the questions we send their way. Is God, in some sense—or at some times—such a reality, enormous and resplendent but of a kind that does not speak?

Simultaneously—despite my suspicion that written arguments, however cogent and eloquent, cannot transmit faith—you might begin to read the thoughts of the prime believing minds. I've already suggested Augustine and Francis of Assisi. Beyond them—for you, friend, with your origins in Christianity—those potent minds would draw you toward the words of Jesus as preserved in the four canonical gospels (and the ancient Gospel of Thomas, discovered intact only some sixty years ago, is well worth your attention). Then you might launch yourself on a knowledge of the lives and works of heroic and exemplary—and more contemporary—believing figures like Søren Kierkegaard, Albert Schweitzer,

Simone Weil, W. H. Auden, Dorothy Day, Flannery O'Connor, and Walker Percy. Those are only a small handful of the almost inexhaustible library which patiently awaits modern readers.

Here it's worth stressing a sad reality which I mentioned earlier. One of the problems you'll likely face as you study the life of Jesus is a gradual awareness that any public mention of him, his teachings, and his sane followers in present-day America, may well engender an immediate and inflexible opposition to the very sound of his name. So much hypocrisy and hate have been peddled in that name, so much harm continues to be done, that a degree of initial opposition is easily comprehensible. Jesus, in short, is unfairly blamed for the appalling errors of a great many of his followers.

But the intensity of that present hostility, which often approaches disdain and sometimes reaches a dreadful level of ferocity, can prove astonishing. Any close attention to the gospel histories of Jesus' life and to his actual words, however—shorn of the uses made of them by his blind or hateful followers—will reveal a human figure who may have made staggering claims for himself but who also displayed a steady and welcoming tolerance and a healing power which renders such opposition from self-described Christians as baffling as any you'll meet in your lifetime.

Second, considering that your family will have reared you in a world deep in the knowledge and resonance of the arts, I'd urge you to immerse yourself in the lives and works of the great believing composers and painters—

such witnesses as the preservers of Gregorian chant, the architects of the medieval cathedrals, their sculptors and stained-glass makers; the art of Giotto and Botticelli and Michelangelo, Rembrandt, Millet and Van Gogh and Rouault; the music of Palestrina and Tallis, Bach and Handel, Mozart and Beethoven, Bruckner, Elgar, Fauré, Messiaen, Barber, Górecki, and Arvo Pärt. None of those believers was, or is, a fool or a mere hired hand of the pope or of some prince with an idle and unadorned chapel. When you read about those makers, you'll see that many of them were tortured in their faith, sometimes approaching disbelief; yet their works remain adamant witnesses to the motive engine of belief.

The vitality and emotional profundity of their art, the skills they employ, and many of the makers' surviving personal statements show them to be intellectually and emotionally tough-minded, trustworthy, and frequently joyful. Beware, then, of thinking—or being led to think—that we've learned anything decisive in recent centuries that renders the convictions of such giants untrustworthy. Not at all incidentally here, I've omitted the whole world of poetry, fiction, and drama. That virtual universe is, if anything, even more bountiful in its offerings than are music, painting, sculpture, and architecture.

The same advice can be given for almost all the world's widespread religions, freighted as they are with glorifications of the mystery and presence and dreaded absence of God, though the artists of Judaism and Islam (because of their prohibitions on the portrayal of living things) have concentrated their findings in visual fantasy and in such non-visual forms as prophecy, poetry, and music. The sacred visual arts and music of Buddhism, Hinduism, and Shinto are immense in quantity; and the sacred arts of sub-Saharan Africa, of African-American and African-Caribbean peoples, and the American Indian are copious, imposing, and remain to be widely known.

While you're reading and listening, you might want to try speaking aloud — if you never have — short sentences to the air around you. Speak low and be sure no one is watching; people have been carted off for less. Call the air *God* if you can, though it's not a god (the name for the Holy Spirit in Greek, though, is *pneuma* — a word which also means *breath* or *wind*). Then state as honestly as possible some immediate need, however trivial — some hope for guidance. Don't be deterred by anyone who asks you how such words might reach God — through sound waves, by telepathic transfer, or however else.

I at least am at ease in the idea that any mind which created the visible universe, if nothing more, could surely have arranged to be contacted by his creatures if he wished to hear them. And the modern computer, with its phenomenal resources of memory, may provide the only model we need for imagining that the Creator can attend to all his creatures simultaneously and can process their needs — again, if he chooses to do so. Continue your words then, audible or silent; and with luck and further effort, your sentences will grow less self-obsessed. They may even begin to express occasional thanks for what I hope will be a good life.

For long months you may get no trace of notice or reply from the air you've addressed. The saints, and normal believers afflicted with melancholia and psychosis, have often waited through appalling years of silence. A tragic band of the psychotic seem to hear an awful inner gabble which they sometimes call God—and even demons—but is almost surely neither. Eventually, however, you may hear answers to your own questions on a scale as valid and useful for your own life, and those that surround you, as any communications received by the spiritual masters I've named.

And if an answer comes, try assuming for a while that it wasn't simply the air that answered you. We constantly make such assumptions in the silent stretches that mark our relations with our living kin, friends, and enemies. We often endure long gaps of careless or antagonized silence from those human creatures, we interpret the meaning of those gaps, and very often we're right. Why not make such an assumption in one's attempt at communicating with God?

There are numerous possible next steps. You might want to begin frequenting spaces that have a natural benignity for you—whether it's a picture of the lobby of the now-destroyed Penn Station in New York, Michelangelo's austere Medici Chapel in Florence, the Birth Cave beneath the altar of the Church of the Nativity in Bethlehem, the Dome of the Rock in Jerusalem, the Taj Mahal in India, a quiet neighborhood church, or a one-man firewatch tower high above a primal forest. You might begin to talk about your findings with some friend whom you suspect of having similar curiosities. Be careful at this point about consulting believers who are vividly and publicly enthusiastic (an adjective that means possessed by a god, which is not always a bad thing but which bears careful watching). By premature celebration of what they take to be a friend's first successes, they've terminated more nascent faith than they've fostered.

You might now begin to commit some part of your time to working with the wretched of your city block or small town—the homeless and hungry, the abused, the unloved whom most religions insist that we comfort (and whom some believers suggest may occasionally be inhabited by a watchful god in disguise). It was Salinger's Zooey Glass who revealed to his troubled sister Franny that "the Fat Lady is Jesus." If Zooey was even partly right, there are many more candidates for care and worship than there used to be. If you think you can sustain your sanity in the face of hard assaults, you might want to work with the truly outcast—the insane and filthy, the apparently demonic. I was never strong enough, or unselfish enough, to do so; but I'd almost surely be a better man if I had been.

You might want to try attending some regular religious ceremony—a Catholic mass, a Protestant Sunday-morning service, a black revival with rapturous music. Again, I've told you how I departed from formal

religious services early in my manhood and how I've since come to feel that my work and my private devotions have translated themselves, quite seriously, into the two forms of worship that come near to answering my own spiritual needs and to freeing up whatever gifts I have to offer my fellow creatures and God—in my writing and my classrooms (my classes, incidentally, are apparently very unsacred seeming—in any case, they're accompanied by a good deal of laughter, serious and silly).

I've worked to guarantee that my keen-eyed fearless students and the critics of my writing correct any excessively prideful tendencies that might otherwise have been dealt with in an honest religious congregation. Don't read me entirely wrong, though. I'm not necessarily an enemy of churches and synagogues, mosques and temples. If they can truly help you, and you them—if you can avoid the hypocrisy and self-satisfaction and sometimes hatred that they so frequently foster—so much the better. Goodness has surely come from them, along with enormous quantities of blinding purple gas and spilled blood.

I'm speaking in the terms of my own lifelong faith

◀ *The lobby of Penn Station was my introduction to New York on my arrival by train in November 1950. It struck me at once as one of humankind's prime achievements; and that far at least, I was right. The fact that it would be willfully destroyed only thirteen years later is among the appalling realities of American greed.* (Bettman/Corbis)

and your family's. I'm very far from implying that other faiths are not worthy roads to a common destination. And I'm especially far from thinking that there's no salvation outside Christianity, much less a particular denomination. For all the beauty of the truth of God's incarnating himself in the one man Jesus, an equally enormous fact is that it's a disastrous insult to God's immensity and final inscrutability to confine him to a single mode of belief, a single name and body. And when Jesus says, in the Gospel of John's version of the last supper, "No one comes to the Father but through me," I'd note first that he's speaking to the disciples, not at all necessarily to me and his later followers. Then I'd wonder, as I do about so many of John's reported sayings, whether or not these excluding words can have come from the historical Jesus and not from John's own rich imagination and his apparent enmity toward the synagogues from which he and his own followers, near the end of the first century, had felt expelled.

In fact, long observation has suggested to me that someone who has an early grounding in one particular faith may be at serious peril if he or she later attempts to switch allegiance and go elsewhere. I've known a good many very confused believers who've switched track once or more in their adult lives. If the ceremonies of your own faith fail you, don't assume that the fault is your own. Don't indulge in self-congratulation either. Don't assume for a moment that you're smarter, more tasteful, or morally superior to anyone you've encountered in such a community (though there's sometimes a chance that you may be). Go back to yourself and the quiet ambient air and try to wait with whatever degree of calm care you can manage.

Soon or late, you'll likely get some response from that space to which you first spoke. It may say what it's said to many good people in many centuries—*There's nothing here but atoms of air. Stop waiting and get yourself an unpropped life.* It's possible that, should there be anything in the immensity of space beyond you, it may always refuse to reply. Surely nothing could be more daunting for a seeker, though millions have faced such a blank-wall exclusion and gone on to live decent, sometimes heroic lives.

But then the force, whom most humans trust in some form or other, may say to you what it has apparently said persuasively to even more of the Earth's human beings than it's ever refused—*Keep talking. Learn how. You're listened to. One day you may hear me again more clearly, should I need or want you. You may even sometime see me in one of my infinite forms.*

The Lord Krishna shows his multiple forms, in terror and splendor, at Arjuna's request in the most astonishing moment of the Hindu Bhagavad Gita—

> "I am come as Time, the destroyer of people,
> Ready for the hour that ripens to their ruin."

The tribal god of the Hebrews shows his back to Moses on Mount Sinai in the Book of Exodus; and then he both names and describes himself as he marches past, partly visible but cloaked in ultimate strangeness —

"Yahweh, Yahweh, a loving God, kind, slow to anger, full of mercy and truth, keeping mercy for thousands, forgiving wrong and trespass and sin but not entirely leaving guilt unpunished, visiting the wrong of fathers on children, on children of children to the third and fourth generation."

In the Gospel of Mark, Jesus takes the three disciples of his innermost circle, leads them up a high mountain (probably Mount Hermon), moves some distance away, and then reveals himself, transfigured in dazzling radiance as God's Son —

He was changed in shape before them and his garments became a very shining white such as no bleacher on Earth can whiten. And Elijah appeared to them with Moses and they were talking with Jesus.

If you read the remainder of that transfiguration in Mark's gospel you will see that Jesus' pupils who witnessed such a moment proved initially terrified and confused to the point of absurdity. Ultimately these plain Galilean fishermen rallied most powerfully however, and what they'd seen carried them onward through martyrdom (in at least two of their cases) toward the eventual spiritual conquest of the Roman empire. Thus as I mentioned above, God or his various messengers are reported to have visited otherwise unexceptional men, women, and children throughout known history with surprising news delivered in voices they can hear and, at least partially, comprehend.

If you choose, you may, in short—and finally, my honored young friend—attempt to speak with and to hear from what may be the core of truth, in our universe at least. In the fourth century Augustine said—and he's been, after Paul, the most influential theologian of the West—"Since it is God we are speaking of, you do not understand it. If you could understand it, it would not be God."

Nor does anyone else understand it of course (I take it that when Augustine says *it*, he is speaking of the totality of God himself, not of God's communications to us). But the Creator has seldom ceased to send messengers; and a great many human beings—some of them madmen, but some others who're thoroughly clear in the head—remain convinced that they hear God's will in a form that at least resembles communication.

Nothing of course is more dangerous to believe than such a hearing of direct divine will. Yet no other possibility on Earth may be ignored at greater peril to one's self and others. I don't mean to imply that all news which appears to come from God is truly from him. But those words that appear to come from God must be

examined with the closest possible care. I'd encourage you then to persist, though sanely—above all, distrusting each word the moment it hints at awarding you power over any other human life or mind.

To distrust is not necessarily to discard; but when you think you hear some command to alter another creature's life, you've almost certainly heard a voice other than God's. He almost certainly has no need of you to change other lives. He's been doing that on his own, quite adequately, since time began. With sane persistence and serious care, you may one day achieve the complex privilege won by the noblest lives of our species—stretches of actual time on a clock in which you break through to and speak, in a richly usable way, with (of all truly unimaginable contacts) some form of the inexhaustible truth that wears so many fearsome masks for its likely sole face.

If I'm wrong in all I've said above—and I grant the chance—I doubt I'll have done you greater harm than to urge you to take yourself and your whole world as earnestly as, plainly, you and it deserve to be. There are several millennia of voices stronger, maybe truer than

---

◄ *The Taj Mahal in Agra, India. Built by Shah Jahan in the seventeenth century as a memorial to his beloved wife— Mumtaz Mahal—who died in childbirth, it is surely the world's most beautiful tomb and one of the grandest shrines of Islam.* (Bettmann/Corbis)

mine. For now, though, this is what I feel compelled to give you — if for nothing else, then as a grave sign of your young life's promise and the weight of your coming significance when, or whether, you come to read this.

> Yours in hope, in any case,
> Reynolds

FURTHER READING, LOOKING, AND LISTENING

In the text above, I've suggested reading as deeply as possible in the Bible—the Hebrew books commonly called the Old Testament and the Christian books called the New Testament. The famous King James translation of 1611 remains an unsurpassed monument of English prose eloquence, but it is based upon what are now known to be frequently untrustworthy Hebrew and Greek texts. There are several admirable later translations presently available. The Revised Standard Version remains my personal favorite, for clarity and loyalty to the original languages. The Revised Standard may prove difficult to find now (it's increasingly been replaced by the New Revised Standard Version, which is misleadingly free in far too many places); but it can be easily located for sale on the Internet or in a large secondhand bookstore. Among other recent translations, I recommend only the widely available New International Version. You can, of course, learn Hebrew and Greek and read the startling originals.

Hurlbut's Story of the Bible, the book that was so important in my own childhood is still in print, though in revised, "simplified" form and with prettified and misleading new illustrations. The old version, which I knew as a child, is available from used-book stores and from the Internet. I buy copies whenever I see them on eBay and entrust them to the children I know.

The central religious texts of other major world religions are represented by the Koran, the Bhagavad Gita (a stand-alone component of the immensely long Sanskrit epic, the Mahabharata), and various collections of the Buddha's teachings. I read the Koran in a Penguin edition translated by N. J. Dawood. I read the Bhagavad Gita in several translations but find the Prabhavananda/ Isherwood translation the most memorable; and while there are numerous other collections of the Buddha's teachings, I read them in a collection called *The Buddhist Tradition* edited by W. T. de Bary. A useful summary guide to all these concerns may be found in a single volume, *The World's Religions* by Huston Smith.

I've mentioned some of the great Christian theologians—Paul of Tarsus and Augustine, prime among them. The letters of St. Paul, those which are authentic and those of dubious authorship, are found in the New Testament (the Christian portion of the Bible).

Augustine's two central works are his *Confessions* and his mammoth, and continuously fascinating, *City of God*. They are available in various translations of Augustine's Latin. *The Little Flowers of St. Francis* can also be read in numerous versions of the Italian original.

Given my lack of serious knowledge of the theology of religions other than my own, I'll decline here to offer recommendations for further reading. If theological speculation interests you, and you come from one of those older traditions, I suggest that you find a well-informed elder to guide you further inward. Since all theologies are speculations of varying degrees of inspiration or lunacy, you'll be well-advised to proceed with a high degree of watchfulness.

The most enduring religious novel known to me, and one of the greatest novels I know of, is unconcealed in its concerns—*The Diary of a Country Priest* by Georges Bernanos, a convincing first-person account of the life of a French priest who has no idea that he's an actual saint. Graham Greene's *The Heart of the Matter* and *The Power and the Glory* are especially arresting and useful, but virtually any of Greene's many novels will prove saturated with concealed religious concerns. Evelyn Waugh's *Brideshead Revisited* is a slowly riveting study of the denial of God by various English characters, rich and poor, through the middle years of the twentieth century. The beauty of its prose alone seems one more demonstration of God's existence (and the lengthy televised version of the novel—presently available on DVD—is almost as revealing and moving). Walker

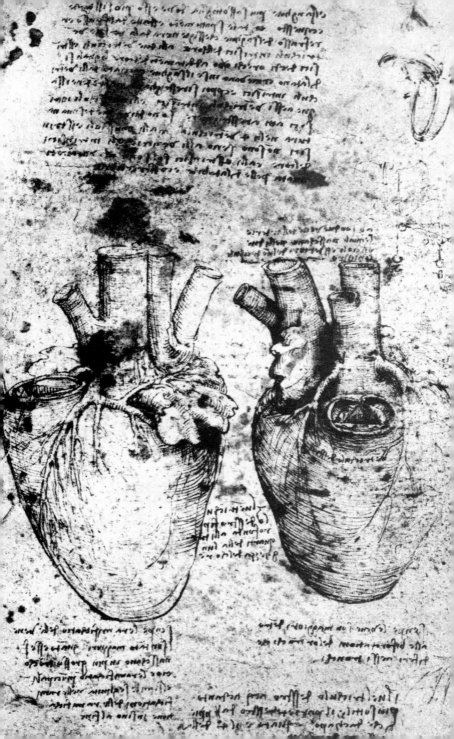

Percy's *The Moviegoer* is a distinguished novel, set largely in New Orleans, with buried religious concerns. The first volume of John Updike's Rabbit series—*Rabbit, Run*—is a moving look at one particular and initially likable American life deprived, for whatever reasons, of divine grace (the remaining three volumes of the Rabbit tetralogy are a painful-to-read look at a family deliquescing in the wastes of a spiritual desert into which they've stumbled with half-open eyes). My own fiction, especially the third novel of my *Great Circle* trilogy—*The Promise of Rest*—is likewise curious about the possibility of divine presence, and absence, in contemporary lives and about their effects upon credible characters in late twentieth-century America. Marilynne Robinson's *Gilead*, another first-person account of the life of a good man who's also a small-town minister, stands with Bernanos's *Country Priest* in its tranquil eloquence and its gathering power.

Illustrations in the text above depict a few of the buildings which have deepened my sense of a Creator. The painters and sculptors whom I mention may be

---

◄ *A drawing by Leonardo da Vinci of the human heart. The question of Leonardo's faith is debatable, but a great deal of his art is devoted to sacred subjects. His numerous anatomical drawings—the result of a pioneering study of human corpses—testify to the phenomenal complexity of our bodies, a reality which some believers fold into their dossiers on faith.* (Bettmann/Corbis)

seen, if not in their home sites, in any number of easily accessible picture books.

The music I've commended may likewise be heard on a shifting wealth of CDs and DVDs and on a diminishing number of FM radio stations. A recommendation of particular performances would be subject to wide variations in taste—and on the very shaky availability of a given disc (musical recordings go out of print even more maddeningly often than books). Again, I recommend the immense riches of the Internet as a source— its auction sites are especially lively and rich in their offerings.

As a listening start from older music, I recommend a selection from the great plenty of Gregorian chant and the masses of Giovanni Palestrina. At the most difficult time in my own life, I listened many times to Francesco Cavalli's *Messa Concertata*. Among more modern works, the B minor Mass of Bach is as inescapable as are the greatest oratorios of Handel—*Israel in Egypt*, say, and *Messiah*. More modern works which insist upon themselves are the *Missa Solemnis* of Ludwig van Beethoven as well as his late string quartets and those of Franz Schubert (who died at thirty-one but composed unforgettably almost to his last breath). The blazing *Requiem* of Giuseppe Verdi is as instructive as it is both frightening and consolatory (the *Requiem* of Gabriel Fauré is as gentle as Verdi is dramatic). Among contemporary composers Henryk Górecki's Third Symphony and Arvo Pärt's *Passio* are powerful in very different ways (Górecki is a religious man, though the Third Symphony is not specifically religious).

In the text I've mentioned other composers, all of whom are well worth searching out and are usually available to the avid hunter. There are literally dozens more — even hundreds more — composers who will inform you, entertain you, and perhaps save your soul (if nothing else does or can). My own choices are clearly from a wing of the vast treasury of music which we generally call classical. My training and my temperament have led me in that direction. I'm more than aware that there are numerous other kinds of music that may prove of greater relevance and long-term use to other earnest seekers (I've long felt, for instance, that one of the great religious songs in modern history is the Beatles' "Let It Be," as performed by them or — shortly thereafter — by Aretha Franklin). If those seekers have not already made their own discoveries, I'd urge them to begin to do so.

In the end here, and despite the sometimes baffling richness of choice and the elusiveness of many desired CDs and tapes — or whatever form of delivery is on hand when you read this — I assert once more the supreme value of music as the art which has most nearly delivered divinity to us.

REYNOLDS PRICE

Reynolds Price was born in Macon, North Carolina in 1933. Educated at Duke University and, as a Rhodes Scholar, at Merton College, Oxford University, he has taught at Duke since 1958 and is now James B. Duke Professor of English.

His first short stories, and many later ones, are published in his *Collected Stories*. *A Long and Happy Life* was published in 1962 and won the William Faulkner Award for a best first novel. *Kate Vaiden* was published in 1986 and won the National Book Critics Circle Award. *The Good Priest's Son* in 2005 was his fourteenth novel. Among his thirty-seven volumes are further collections of fiction, poetry, plays, essays, and translations. Price is a member of both the American Academy of Arts and Letters and the American Academy of Arts and Sciences, and his work has been translated into seventeen languages.